PERCY'S PIECE OF THE WAR

First published in 2010
by Woodfield Publishing Ltd
Bognor Regis ~ West Sussex ~ England ~ PO21 5EL
www.woodfieldpublishing.co.uk

© Percy Shipperbottom, 2010

All rights reserved.
No part of this publication may be reproduced
or transmitted in any form or by any means,
electronic or mechanical, nor may it be stored
in any information storage and retrieval system,
without prior permission from the publisher.

The right of Percy Shipperbottom
to be identified as Author of this work
has been asserted in accordance with
the Copyright, Designs and Patents Act 1988

ISBN 1-84683-107-5

Cover artwork by Kirsten Todd

Percy's Piece of the War

Exploits of an RAF High Speed Launch Wireless Operator in the UK and Far East during the Second World War

PERCY SHIPPERBOTTOM

Woodfield Publishing Ltd

Woodfield Publishing Ltd
Bognor Regis ~ West Sussex ~ England ~ PO21 5EL
tel 01243 821234 ~ **e/m** info@woodfieldpublishing.co.uk

Interesting and informative books on a variety of subjects

For full details of all our published titles, visit our website at
www.woodfieldpublishing.co.uk

*This book is dedicated
to the memory of
Colin Peter Shipperbottom,
who showed such courage
during his illness*

'The Sea Shall Not Have Them'.
(RAF Air Sea Rescue Motto)

~ CONTENTS ~

About the Author iii
Introduction v
Preface vii
1. Before the War 1
2. Joining Up 5
3. France 7
4. Back to England 9
5. Dover 13
6. Ramsgate and HSL 120 15
7. My First Trip 19
8. A Lucky Mistake 21
9. A Few Memorable Pick-Ups 23
10. Just Married 25
11. Meeting the Enemy 27
12. More Incidents 31
13. Fatherhood and an Overseas Posting 33
14. Arrival in India 37
15. Calcutta 39
16. Sea Trials and Tribulations 43
17. Chittagong and the Arakan 45
18. Unfriendly Fire 49
19. On Hill Party 51
20. Lost at Sea 55
21. The CO's Exploits 57
22. A Dangerous Assignment 59
23. Direction Finding 61
24. The Last Days of War 63
25. Homeward Bound 65
26. A Civilian Again 69
    Glossary of Naval Terminology 71
    Epilogue 73

About the Author

Percy Shipperbottom was born in Bolton but spent his childhood in the villages of Affetside and Bradshaw with his Grandad after he and his mother had been abandoned by his father.

Grandad was gamekeeper to Colonel Hardcastle of Bradshaw Hall and had his own cottage deep in 'the Jumbles', then a beautiful, wooded valley.

Percy learned the country ways from Grandad, including how to handle a gun. He had a number of jobs after leaving school, including farmhand and a spell down a coalmine, but he always felt that, with training, he could achieve something more fulfilling.

He went to night school in the 1930s to learn radio telecommunications and this provided a valuable opening for him into the armed forces as the war clouds were forming over Europe.

This is where, in his own words, he begins his memoir.

Percy Shipperbottom.

Introduction

No exact statistics have been collated but it is estimated that around 25,000 lives were saved by the world coverage (except for US & Canadian coasts) of RAF Air Sea Rescue operations.

Fighter pilots were originally equipped only with lifejackets, unlike RAF bomber crews, whose aircraft also carried inflatable life-rafts. From early 1941 all pilots were given dinghy packs with their parachute harness, enabling more pickups to be made and more lives saved.

Sometimes, after an aerial dogfight above the Channel, the pick-up meant going through minefields. Fortunately, the launches would travel so fast that the mines would pop up harmlessly behind them. Being equipped with guns, they would then use the mines for target practise.

Preface

When my nine-year-old granddaughter Leonie was gathering information and artefacts for her school history project at Whittle-le-Woods C-of-E school about 'The Second World War', she asked me if I had anything to contribute. As I was born after the war, I couldn't help her, but I remembered that my late husband had a few 1940s newspapers he had collected, with dynamic front page headlines about 'VE Day' etc.

Children of Whittle-le-Woods C of E School dressed as World War 2 evacuees for their history project, playing the traditional game of tiddlywinks.

I searched these out and between the papers I found the story contained in this book, written and perfectly typed up by Percy Shipperbottom, my husband's late father, which I was not aware existed, although I do remember giving Percy my old typewriter about 25 years ago.

Percy is relating memories of his wartime service to his son and although he wasn't involved in any hand-to-hand fighting, being a radio operator, what an interesting piece it is. It is written lightly, not focusing on the terrible conditions in India and the boundaries of Burma where Percy suffered bouts of malaria, lost his hair and many teeth through disease and poor nutrition. Instead the story humanises the war in many ways, so much so that at times Percy seems to be more concerned about finding his way around than being shot at on the Air Sea Rescue Launch he served aboard.

He relates his service adventures, but also domestic situations, such as not knowing where he lived on his return at the end of the war, due to his family having moved house. Today people would find it hard to imagine life without fast communications – a mobile phone – or any phone!

Percy's account has been left unchanged, therefore the anomalies in grammar remain and the story contains some 'politically incorrect' terminology by present standards, though not at the time, so that also has been left unchanged.

Janet Shipperbottom, 2010

My special thanks to Kirsten Todd, Percy's granddaughter – a graphic designer and illustrator – for the front cover design and illustrations.

1. Before the War

When I ask myself, "where shall I start?" I answer a daft answer to a daft question. "At the beginning". But where is the beginning? In this case, Son, I would say about 1937. At that time I was a boilerman fireman (firebeater) at Bradshaw Bleachworks.

I was earning good money but I was always on the lookout for a better job. That was when I saw an advert put in the paper by Marconi Co. for telegraphists to work on ships and aircraft. Applicants must hold the Post Master General's first class certificate. Strangely enough, next to that advert was one put in by the Northern Counties Radio & Wireless School Preston, offering courses to day and evening students. I decided to have a go at that, and enrolled for evening tuition. Hours seven to nine pm. This suited me fine. To travel from Bolton (or Bradshaw) to Preston was no problem to a keen motorcyclist, which I was at the time.

I was advised to buy two textbooks. The Admiralty Handbook upon magnetism and electricity, radio waves, sound waves, valves and their components and hosts of other things. Ohms Law, Lenz's Law, Faraday's Law, Kirchoff's Law, etc, etc. Volumes one and two. Besides trying to swallow that, I had to learn to send and receive Morse. Fortunately, I had learned the Morse Code in the scouts, but this was another kettle of fish.

Anyway, I battled valiantly on in 1937, 38, 39. By then I could send and receive Morse about 28 words a minute. I had been advised to buy the Postmaster's General Handbook for wireless operators. In that was essential information on the sending and receiving of messages to and from ships or aircraft and the codes etc. Also a code which we was advised to become very familiar with i.e. The Q Code. When the Americans entered the war, my knowledge of the Q code stood me in good stead where a lot of RAF operators had stumbled a bit at first. The British Forces, Army, Navy and Air Force each had their own code but when the Yanks came, the Q code was the thing to learn. Luckily I had a good smattering of it, and even now can remember the three main questions.

But to get back to basics. (I've been dying to get that in).

With the threat of war coming ever closer, I told my mother and Grandad that I was going to choose my job in the Forces.

First I went to the Army, and was doing fine until they asked me what I did and when I told them, they lost interest in me.

So I went to the Navy - same results, only they told my why – I was in a reserved occupation. This knowledge cheered me up, because now I knew what to say when I went to the RAF. I told them I was a general labourer.

They wrote everything down and said that they would send for me.

I went back to work and one day, two weeks later, my mother came to the firehole (boiler house) with a letter. She gave it to me saying, "A chap in a blue uniform riding a motorbike left this."

It was from the RAF, saying my presence was needed at once if not sooner.

I went back in the firehole, got my spade, and with a piece of chalk wrote 'To Let' on it, and leaned it against the boilers I had been working on.

Then I went to the office of the works engineer and asked him for a note to get my cards and my pay. He asked me why and when I told him I had been called up by the RAF.

He said he could easily get me off that, because I was in a reserved occupation.

I told him not to try. If I hid behind a reserved job, I would not feel able to look our Wilf, Grandad or our Jim in the face again.

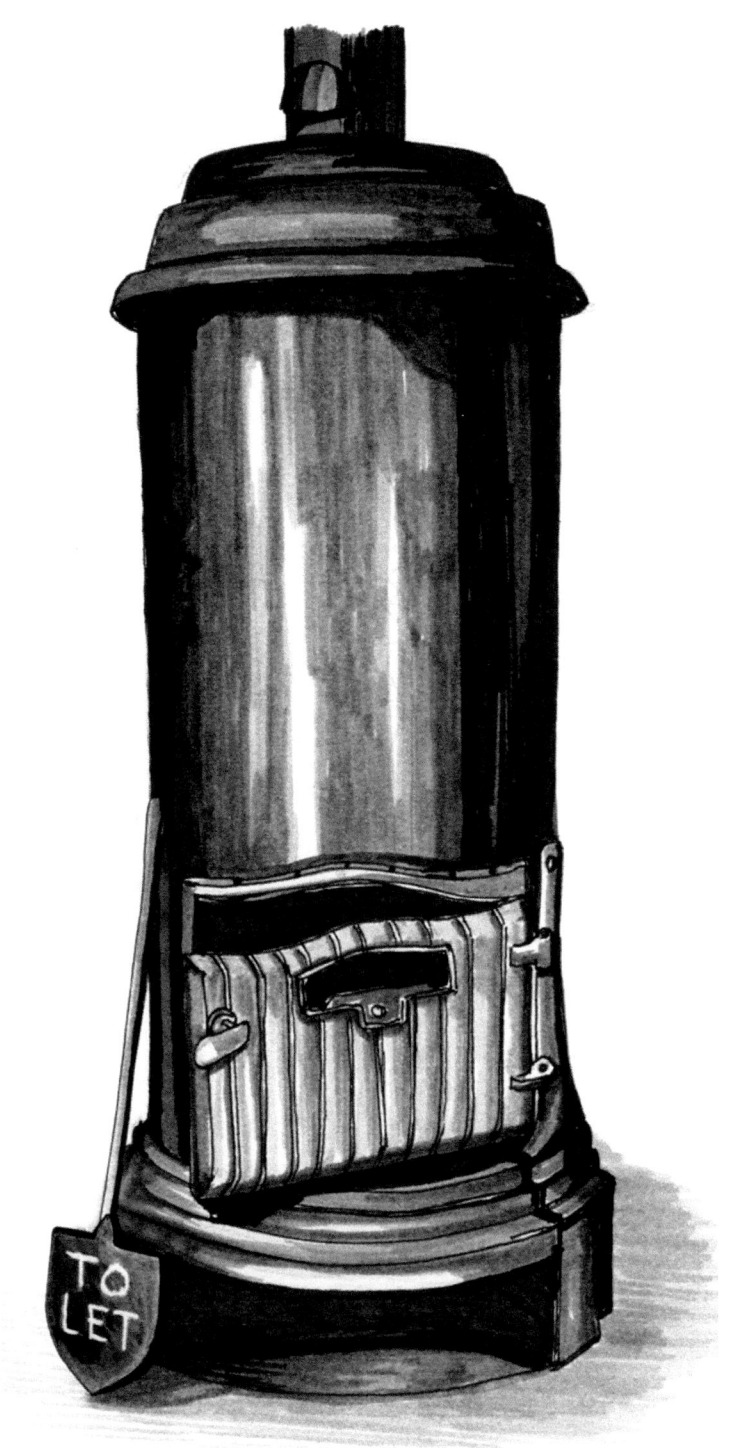

One boilerman's spade to let…

2. Joining Up

Well! That was it and September 1ˢᵗ 1939 I reported to Padgate.

There we were put in the charge and care of a corporal who took a lot of trouble to introduce the ways of the RAF to us.

The second day, we were assembled in a hall and onto the stage at one end of the room came the camp commander, a few other officers and a few other station personnel.

An Officer introduced the C.O. who then stood up, made us welcome and then said, "In a few moments you will be asked to take the oath of allegiance, then you will receive the King's Shilling and a day's pay. Once you have done that you will belong to the RAF, and RAF Rule and Law. Remember, you are all volunteers, you are not conscripted, so you will have a few minutes to think it over, and if any of you wish to change your mind, you can walk out and no one will stop you".

No one walked out.

A bit of 'square bashing' and then we were posted to various schools.

One last bit of humour at Padgate. On Sept. 3ʳᵈ the war was declared and we was square bashing when the air-raid sirens went. We stood looking at the drill corporal in charge of us and he looked like he didn't know what to do. Then "Don't panic!" he shouted and ran like hell to the air raid shelter, followed by his lambs. By the time the air raid shelter was reached, the 'all clear' sounded.

My next school was the gunnery school at Manby, Lincs. There I was taught all about Browning, the Vickers, Lewis, the .22mm.cannon and various other things.

Then came the time for the 'Posting'.

3. France

Three or four of us was called up before the CO, who told us we were being posted to a place called Heston to form a new squadron for France.[1] He said that we would be the first VR squadron in France.

All very nice, but only that morning I had written to my mother and what friends I knew who hadn't been called up, saying I would be home for Christmas.

By then I was on the Marne, where we spent the next six months or so until the very unfriendly Germans made us move, very fast.

We packed what we could into lorries and the officer in charge discovered that he was now in charge of more vehicles than drivers. I happened to be the nearest 'erk' to him and he asked me if I could drive.

Foolishly replying that I could, he told me to "get in that and drive it." 'That' being a Dodge truck I had never seen before.

Some hours later, and a nightmare journey made worse by the French population being in one hell of a panic and blocking the roads, we arrived at an airstrip just outside Orleans, where, I was later informed, our vehicles and contents was destroyed by anti-tank fire.

For a whole day we was like lost sheep.

When I saw the German aircraft flying unopposed and attacking the refugees choking the roads, I said to myself, "God help England".

---

[1] On 10 February 1940, No.212 Squadron was formed at Heston to carry out strategic photographic reconnaissance duties in France, working closely with the Photographic Development Unit. It was intended to have three detachments each of three Spitfires but in the absence of sufficient camera-equipped Spitfires, No.212 was equipped with Blenheims. After flying some operational missions, the detachment in France was forced to evacuate its base on 14 June 1940, and the squadron was absorbed by the Photographic Development Unit on 18 June 1940, which was redesignated the Photographic Reconnaissance Unit on 8 July. (*Source:* RAF official website)

The following day we was still in that one spot, just outside Orleans, so I decided to have a short stroll on the banks of the river Loire. It was wide, slow moving, and I supposed it was deep, but I had no intention of trying to find out.

Whilst I sat there, a very attractive girl smiled and sat down beside me. She said something to me, but I hadn't a clue what it was, so I asked her, in the best French I could muster, if she spoke English.

She informed me she was a refugee of the Spanish Civil War and could only speak English and French very poorly.

Anyway, despite language difficulties, this Spanish girl refugee who spoke French poorly and this English airman who spoke French worse, was proceeding along very nicely and I was beginning to think life could be very interesting if those damn Jerries would leave us alone, when an RAF corporal came dashing down and told me to get a move on as a Kite had flopped down and was ready for take-off.

I made an Olympic style dash to the airfield and had barely got on the Kite (a Lockheed Hudson) before it took off.

My kit and respirator was left to the care of ... WHO?

Across France we flew, and then we picked up a tail. Three ME's and our pilot played hide and seek in the clouds.

As we passed the Channel Isles I was just thinking it might be a bit softer landing in the sea, when we saw three Hurricanes going to entertain our friends.

The rest of the journey, over Cornwall and so on to Heston, was quite a peaceful ride.

4. Back to England

We was given civvy billets and a 48 hour leave pass.

I only had the clothes I stood up in, so the SWO quickly made arrangements for us to be fully kitted out.

I went to my new digs in Cranford Lane and was soon established there.

A quick clean up and change and then I went back to the airfield to see if there was any chance of any money.

I was told I would have to wait for that, but I did not intend to wait.

The pilot who had lifted us out of France had seen I was in possession of a .38 automatic I had obtained from a French airman, and I knew he wanted it. So I found him and said he could have it for £2.

He asked me why that, so I told him that there wasn't much chance of pay just yet, I had a 48 hr pass and I intend to go home. I said that Thirty Bob on the train would leave Ten for a drink.

He smiled, gave me the money, saying "have a good leave" and I gave him the pistol and 50 rounds of ammo.

Back in Bolton I quickly did the rounds.

On my way to see Grandad I called at the Works to see an old friend of mine who was in charge of the boiler house and had written to me when I was in France.

He told me to go to the office because they had some money which was due to me. This I did and got a nice handy sum of money.

Then I went to see Grandad and was surprised to see our Wilf there. He had joined the RAF (Balloons) and was on leave. So we went to town, visiting all our favourite pubs where we drank well and FREELY, in every sense, and every pub gave us some money out of the 'Soldiers Box'.

But all good things come to an end, and our Wilf said he would have to go back on the Friday, so that was the day I decided to go back and take whatever punishment was coming to me for being a few days adrift.

That was the only time in my RAF service that I returned to my unit richer than when I left!

On arrival at Heston I reported to the SWO (Station Warrant Officer) and was surprised to see it wasn't the same SWO I had reported to before.

He asked me who I was and who I belonged to.

I told him my number, rank and name and that I belonged to 212 Squadron.

Then, to my surprise, he asked if I had had B.E.F. leave.

I told him, quite truthfully, I had not. Whereupon he made me make out a leave pass, which he signed, then gave me a rail warrant to Bolton and a note to pay office for the pay due to me and ration cards.

I caught the same train back to Bolton I had come down on.

When I returned I found a different set up. 212 Squadron had been swallowed up into a new outfit called P.R.U. (Photographic Reconnaissance Unit) and I was in C flight, with A Flight in Wick and B Flight in St. Eval. Flights to change round every three months.

But it didn't quite work out that way. Wherever PRU went, Jerry seemed to think we made a good target. I did a stint at Heston – that was when I met Joan, your Mam, at a dance at the Red Lion, Hounslow.

I did a stint at Wick, and instead of Heston, we moved out to the wilds of Oxfordshire, but Jerry still found us. Whilst there I was posted to Compton Basset, a radio school where I was brought up to scratch on WT Procedure also on RDF (Radio Direction Finding).

The course finished, we looked at the notice board to see what was in store for us. To my surprise I was posted to RAF Dover.

I puzzled, wondering what sort of squadron would be at Dover.

Bomber, I thought.

Anyway, I had a seven-day leave due, so made quick tracks to Hounslow, because I wanted Joan to come with me and see Lancashire without frills.

This was accomplished, and so I was ready to see what Dover had for me.

Joan

5. Dover

What a start and what a surprise!

The train was frequently stopped and held up by shelling. Jerry was lobbing shells across the Channel. The result was, instead of arriving at ten PM the train pulled in about 11.45 pm.

Then I had to find RAF Dover.

Fortunately a local policeman gave me precise instructions or I would have spent the night wandering about Dover in a very tight blackout. I would not have known the RAF was in a damn big school almost on top of the harbour.

I wandered into the school, and saw an RAF Service Police Officer. He took me to the duty SWO. I gave him my papers, including my leave pass which he scrutinised like he was looking at some rare gem, then said, "You could be on a charge. You've overstayed your leave and you are adrift."

I looked at him in amazement.

"What does it say on that pass?" I asked.

"It says 23.59 yesterday, it is now 00.20 hrs today."

I looked at him. "Have you travelled 200 bloody miles on the train since this bloody war broke out?"

"Come on," he said, "I'll show you a bed. Breakfast at 8, I'll take you to the CO at nine".

Right on nine a.m. I was shown into the C.O.'s office. He was a Wing Commander. To me he looked rather elderly and if he had told me he was in the RAF when Robin was a Hood, I would have believed him. Instead, he asked me about my Service up to date, and when I had told him, he surprised me by asking me if I enjoyed sailing.

I told him I really did enjoy sailing.

He asked me if I had done much and I said "Oh Yes", thinking about my vast experience on the Isle of Man boats.

"Good" he said.

He wrote something on a piece of paper and gave it to me saying, "Take this to the orderly room. They will give you a bus pass to Ramsgate. When you get to Ramsgate, make your way to the Naval Base, it is easy to find and anyone in the Base will tell you where the RAF Orderly room is. The bus station here is just outside the building so you will have no problem on that."

He just gave me a sort of smile, and I took that as a dismissal.

Giving him a smart salute I left the room and made my way to the orderly room. A cheerful WAAF gave me a bus pass and said I would have no problems with the bus.

She was right and in a very short time, I was on my way to Ramsgate.

6. Ramsgate and HSL 120

On arrival the bus conductor told me how to get to the Naval Base and soon I was asking a naval rating the way to the RAF orderly room. Actually, I was almost next to it. Up a short flight of steps, and there it was.

I knocked on the door and entered a cosy little room with two tables and about six chairs. At the first table near the door sat two airmen. I soon learned that one was a clerk GD (General Duties) the other was a clerk Pay Bob (Accounts). True to tradition, I knew he was the one I would count among my friends.

At the other table sat a Flight Sergeant and a Flight Lieutenant, who, between them controlled the small bunch of RAF bodies in that base. They were known to all simply as 'Chiefy Grace' and 'Daddy Haines'.

The Flight Sergeant said to the officer, after looking at my papers, "Sir, this is the replacement wireless op".

The C.O. looked at my papers and in a very friendly voice, asked, "Have you ever done any sailing?"

I said that I had done a little and at the same time I wondered why it was so important about having done some sailing.

I was soon to find out.

The clerk GD was told to show me my bed space, where I was to eat and then, when I had dumped my kit, he was to take me to "one twenty".

What "one twenty" was I was soon to find out.

My 'bed space' was a hammock, slung and lashed Navy fashion, my kit stowed on the floor below it. I learned that we ate with the Navy, did things Navy style and came under Naval Discipline for lots of things. Then my guide said, "Now, I will take you to one twenty".

Walking along the harbour wall, he stopped and, pointing to a motor boat moored alongside another, he said, "There you are, that's yours, the 120. The W.O.P. onboard will put you wise."

I went down some steps and onto the boat, officially known as HSL 120 (High Speed Launch 120).[2]

Onboard was a wireless operator and when he saw me he started dashing about, gathering things together and putting them all in a bag.

When he was satisfied that he had all he wanted, he turned to me and said, "Right, it's all yours."

I asked him what he was doing and in a very Geordie accent said, "I'm away home."

I asked him if he was going on leave and he said "Am I bloody 'ell! I've finished. Out the bloody RAF."

I asked if he was going on compassionate grounds or something and he said, "No, I'm a miner, an I'm gooin' back to the pit".

Strangely enough, some eighteen months later, I was approached by a pinstripe bowler hat type in the base office and he asked me if I wanted to go back to the mine.

I told him I had left a reserve job AFTER I had left the mine and if I had wanted to stay at the pit, I wouldn't have left in the first place.

Then he said that I could be *made* to go back.

"Look!" I said, "It's cost the RAF about £600 to train me. I've no desire to go back to the pit or any other job whilst this war is on. You make me, if you

---

[2] HSL 120 was one of the RAF 100 class High Speed Launches, which began to join the RAF fleet in 1937. Built by The British Power Boat Company at Hythe, the wooden-hulled 100 class HSLs were designed by Fred Cooper. The launches were 64ft long with a beam of 14ft and powered by a trio of 500 horsepower Napier Sea Lion engines they were capable of a top speed of 39 knots. Only 22 were in service and HSL 120 was the last but one to be built.

can, but I assure you, that whoever employs me will think he's got a ghost working for him."

Daddy Haines and Chiefy Grace couldn't hide their amusement and Bowler Hat made like he had a train to catch.

Chiefy Grace said, "Right, go back to your boat. I don't think you'll be bothered again."

The launch was one of four based at Ramsgate and was employed on Air Sea Rescue.

I soon realised why I was asked if I had spent any time at sea.

7. My First Trip

I did lots of trips before I went overseas, but that first trip stuck in my mind. The procedure was that if there was any air strikes or bombing, etc, the rescue boats were placed on rendezvous at strategic points along the flight path of the aircraft, so that if a pilot had to 'ditch' there was a good chance that he and his crew, if any, could be saved.

Well! Whilst the boat was moving, it was great, then we got to the R.V. and with engines shut off, we were at the mercy of the waves. I started to feel queasy, and was sure the damn boat was going to turn over.

I lay on the deck and brought up all the food I had eaten in the last two days. When I started to feel a bit better the coxs'n kindly brought me a big bowl of soup with nice big pieces of fat floating in it. No thanks!

In time I got over the sea-sickness and started to enjoy the work. I made some good friends and the arguing and bickering one generally hears in a barrack room, was entirely absent.

The Base was a four board base and Navy style, each boat crew had its own table on the 'Mess Deck', with the shore staff on their own table.

The first day there I felt completely lost after I had been told which boat I was on and I sat in the base whilst others dashed about, those who were not on duty, getting ready to go out.

One chap, a wireless op on one of the other boats, asked me why I wasn't going out. I said that I had just had leave and that sort of makes one a little short of the needful.

He just said, "Forget about that, we've just been paid, I'll stand you a few drinks and show you the delights of Ramsgate. My name is Barney Hughes. Now come on, we'll talk while we drink."

That was the start of one of the best friendships I had in the Forces.

8. A Lucky Mistake

I soon got the pattern of crash calls, so to save time I wrote out the various ways it could come, so that when a call started I only needed to check the heading and I could tell what it would be, so that before the transmission finished, the boat was well underway.

I got quite a good name for being a fast operator, which was what was needed on Air Sea Rescue. I also worked out the various ways we could get the most favourite call of all, i.e. return to base.

But a near slip up on that once earned me great praise and resulted in one of the quickest pick-ups of all time…

We had been laying on R.V. for quite a long time and then the Morse started chattering. I checked the heading 'Return to……..' so I said, "Back to harbour, Sir".

There were several ways a Morse Message could send a launch about its operation or return to harbour. I had worked out most of these standard messages on a list, so that long before the transmission finished, I had only to check the heading and I knew what was to come.

On this day in question, we had been on R.V. for about four hours, when the Morse began, I checked the heading and after the second group of the Code, I knew it was a return to harbour in the text of 'Return to Ramsgate'. So 'Back to Harbour' I told the cox, who told the Skipper.

We were merrily on our way when I decided to check the latter part of the message. The number of groups was right, but the one next to the last did not match what I had encoded out of the book. So decoding that group made me ask Control for a repeat of that group.

I had received it correctly the first time, so then I decided to put all that together and the message read NOT 'Return to Ramsgate' which I had assumed, but 'Return to Sandgate' which was a bloody buoy some miles up the Channel.

To give the impression I had received another separate message, I said to the Coxswain, "Go to Sandgate."

The cox relayed it to the Skipper who made a slight alteration of course.

Hardly had the course been corrected when I received a Crash Call.

Hardly had I handed it to the Cox and then on to the Skipper when the lookout shouted "Dinghy Ahead!"

It was our Crash Call alright. The fastest on record, everyone congratulating everyone else, even the pilot saying how quick we were between his Mayday and our arrival. To quote him, "I hadn't time to get my feet wet."

'Sparks', yours truly, also came in for praise for excellent operating and I thought it a shame to tell them of the clanger I nearly dropped and gloried in the praise.

9. A Few Memorable Pick-Ups

There are a few 'pickups' that stand out from the others, all for different reasons.

One day we picked up a Polish airman. He was an allied airman, so from his 'dog tag' I encoded his number, rank and name and his physical state. In this case uninjured.

Some two or three months later, we picked up a pilot, slightly injured and when I looked at the dog tag I just could not believe it. It was the same bloke we had picked up before.

When I sent the message, and base had accepted it, I said to the Cox, "just watch base ask for a repeat". Almost at once base asked for a repeat, which I sent back slightly slower, which they accepted.

The Cox asked me how I knew that would happen.

I told him I had sent that name not so long ago and base asked for a repetition then.

The Cox asked me why, so I said, "Look at the name, it's a bloody code in itself! I don't know how to pronounce it. Do you?".

He admitted his education did not stretch to that, even if he was in the Thames River Police before the war.

On one call we got almost to the French Coast.

Sometimes to assist, and help speed the pick-up, and if necessary give the rescue launch some protection, base would send 'Aircraft Circling', and generally, in that case, the aircraft would guide us to the spot. So we were not surprised when I received the aircraft circling message. What was surprising was that the aircraft was not the expected fighter, but a damn big bomber. I think it was a Lancaster, I'm not sure now.

Anyway, there he was, slowly circling, and he led us to the airman, almost ashore on the French Coast. He circled whilst we picked the airman up, I pick up the Aldis lamp and flashed 'All OK TKS' (TKS for thanks).

The aircraft circled and flashed 'Going home'.

I flashed 'T' (received) 'TKS'.

Again the aircraft circled and flashed the same message and I acknowledged. This happened three or four times and all the time we were stationary in plain view of the French Coast. In the end, the Skipper asked me what was going on.

I told him the aircraft kept saying he was going home.

We were still stationary in full view of the coast and the Skipper said, "Tell him to f--- off then. He's going to get us blown out the f---ing water!"

"Just as given Sir?" I said.

"Yes!" he said, "and be bloody quick about it!"

So when the aircraft circled again, I flashed the message with the Aldis and he flashed back 'TKS' and the aircraft then made towards our shores.

Up to then our engines had just been idling, but when the two powerful engines, the same type that powered a Spitfire, opened up, some German must have decided we were not on his side and opened fire. A rather long hope, because we were now at full speed and out of range for accurate fire.

10. Just Married

I got a week's leave to marry your Mam and I travelled to Bolton.

At the end of the week I went to see my doctor and told him I had a sore throat and a sick headache. I didn't feel fit to travel back to my Unit and I would like a Doctor's note to cover my absence.

He never examined me or anything but just said, "How long would you like?"

Surprised, I said a week would do.

He just smiled and gave me the note.

Then I sent a telegram to Base with the words, 'Unfit to travel. Doctor's Note following'.

When I did return to base, the C.O., Chiefy Grace, the Skipper, Cox and every Tom, Dick and Harry, including some of the Wrens on the base, had their dig at me about going on leave to get married and being unfit to travel at the end of the week!

11. Meeting the Enemy

Well, it was business as usual and a Crash Call sent us out into the North Sea. The dinghy had in three Germans! One badly injured, one slightly injured and one OK. He was the last onboard and he stood at the stern of the boat and gave the Nazi salute saying "Heil Hitler". One of the M.B.C.s (correct term for launch deck hands, Motor Boat Crew) had a boat hook in his hands which he used to pull the Dinghy onboard, and he swung round with his boat hook knocking the upstart Nazi back into the drink and said to the Skipper, "Reverse Sir".

The Skipper smiled, saying, "I'd like to but it wouldn't look good on the report". So now the very, very wet and cold Nazi was dragged back onboard and pushed into the well deck where he lay very quiet until we were nearly in Ramsgate. It was impressed upon him that, like his two companions, he must take off all his clothes, and put on 'survivor's clothes' which were warm and dry, his other companions having already done so.

This was the usual procedure for all who were rescued irrespective of nationality. The crew then would pick out what they fancied for souvenirs. If there was just a pilot in the dinghy the MBC's would quickly judge the size of the unfortunates boots and the one who was nearest would go in the dinghy to assist. Flying boots were always easy to sell. Of this particular enemy crew, as usual, after those that had actually done the picking up etc. had sorted out what they wanted, the rest of us decided between us who had what. From a flying coat of one of them, I decided to cut out some sort of flying badge sewn onto a sleeve.

That night we went for a drink, leaving the Germans to the tender mercies of the medics. The following morning I reported sick. A violent headache and generally feeling rotten. The Naval medical officer had me rushed off to Ramsgate hospital and in a private ward where he visited me every day for ten days. Then he asked me where my home was, I told him and how far it was. He said I would have to go on ten days sick leave. I had only been back three weeks from leave but he repeated that I was to have ten days leave. I was to go to base and get money, ration cards and get the soonest train out.

I went to the orderly room and when I told Chiefy Grace, he blew his top. He said that no way was I to go on leave again, Bla Bla and so on. I pointed out that it was not my idea, but the Naval Medic's. Picking the phone up he raved, "I'll soon put a stop to that". I stood there, smoking my pipe and listening to poor Chiefy, "But he's just had… Yes Sir, but we can't… Yes Sir. Yes Sir, I'll see to it at once Sir, Bye."

He turned to me and said, "go to the orderly room, get all that you need, I'll have everything ready when you come back. You are not to take any kit with you, I'll have transport ready to take you to the station. Bloody Naval Medics, I just don't believe it!"

What he didn't believe, I was only to learn of from our own launch medic when I returned from 'sick leave'. He told me that after I left, all the crew had to have a bath, the bathwater having a strong injection of a disinfectant, which turned the water pink. All the spoils collected from the German crew were taken and burned.

In the harbour area, barred to all civilians except those with a pass, was a large public house, empty, so someone who I suppose got paid for thinking up bright ideas, thought it would be a good idea if the RAF rescue personnel moved into there for all purposes except eating, therefore we were still on Naval rations. I don't know who thought that one up, but I reckon that was one of the brilliant ideas of those little gods of war, who got paid for thinking up ideas. Most of which was soundly cursed by those unfortunates to whom they applied.

We had moved into this hotel about two weeks before the episode of the Germans and me going sick resulting in a leave. Whilst I was away the whole place was fumigated, including the clothes of the crew that had picked up the Germans. I also learned that the clothes I went on sick leave in was done first whilst I was in hospital. Then the rest was done and stored until I came back. All this our crew medic told me.

It seemed that one of the Germans was a threat of the plague, V.D. or any other form of disaster to the human race. Therefore the big panic. But I never did find out exactly why I got an extra leave through reporting sick with a headache.

Percy (seated) aboard HSL 120.

12. More Incidents

Well! Things settled down to the usual routine, but three instances stand out in my memory before I move on a bit.

The first, a report from the channel patrol of a parachute sighted at a certain position. We soon found the para, and when they pulled it in, in the harness was a dead German and only the harness was holding him together. When they had got him on deck all kinds of sea life came wriggling, crawling and running from him. They got his dog tag and wrapped him up in his para and whilst I transmitted in plain English, so that our German listeners also got the information, 'One German Airman dead' with number and name. A practice we always did. The MBCs got busy with bucket, brush and mop, putting the livestock back in the sea. I have never eaten seafood since.

Some time after we got a call out to the North Sea, and when we got there, we didn't feel all that happy at what we saw. But in the end when we had got it onboard, we looked forward with pleasure at the red faces of someone when they see what they had trailed us out into the North Sea for. The 'Dinghy' we were directed to was a barrage balloon that had broken loose from somewhere.

If the weather was too bad for flying, the administrators of the RAF would inform their Naval counterparts and they in turn would inform us upon the state of alert to be in. i.e. immediate, one minute, five or anything up to one hour, or two hours. After that it was 'Stand off', which meant that we could sleep in our comfortable beds at night.

One such night and after a few drinks, we settled down for a good night's kip. To alert the crews for a call out, a very shrill bell was rung and the system of ringing could get a single boat out, or all out. It was no use to ignore the bell and use the excuse of not hearing it. I think that will be the bell used on resurrection day. Anyway! The bell rang for duty boat and that was us, about two a.m. and we was not pleased. We dressed quickly and ran to the launch. It was pelting down with rain and a wind like a gale, waves breaking over the harbour wall. When we left the harbour and made for the North Sea, I remarked that any bloody pilot daft enough to fly in that weather deserved all he got. That night the sea wasn't rough, it was MURDEROUS. I was surprised that the radio equipment worked. When we had been going just short of an hour, Base decided to cheer us up and sent, 'MTB in your area', I acknowledged it. Then Base called the MTB and told him a HSL was in his area. That was so we wouldn't start shooting at one another in the darkness. Not long after that there was such a bump I thought we had hit the MTB and I went up on deck. We had not collided with anything but was alongside a massive network of steel girders rising way above us. It was known as an anti-invasion fort and manned mostly by marines. One of them had a suspected appendicitis and had radioed for help. Now this thing towered way up above us and I wondered how they were going to get a very sick man from there to the deck. No problem. He was tightly strapped in a Neil Robinson stretcher. Anyway, when we got back to Ramsgate, an ambulance was waiting. We heard that he got well after his operation and was back on fort.

13. Fatherhood and an Overseas Posting

For some time the Skipper and crew knew I was expecting to become a father. Then one day I got a telegram and they wanted to know what it was.

"A Boy". I told them

"You lucky bugger," the Skipper said. "We have to wet its head". So out came the rum (Survivor's Rum issued by the Navy) and then a leave pass.

About three days into my leave I got a telegram. 'Leave extended, six weeks. Overseas posting'.

I went to Ramsgate for my gear and the Skipper said, "Don't worry Sparks, you are not on the boat yet. We've not given up to keep you here".

I went to Dover to get cleared and when I went into the orderly room the clerk said, "So you are Shipperbottom. There have been letters, telephone calls and all sorts to stop your posting. But nobody can stop a records posting. Ramsgate even offered two in your place. I don't know why, or what, but you certainly had some power rooting for you. I wish you all the best mate".

So to the Transit Camp at West Kirby I went and we were told that no one was to leave the camp. There was no booze. So a Flight Sergeant and I decided we must have a last drink in England. So we broke camp. Quite an easy job really, and in the wee small hours we quietly re-entered camp.

The following morning we was bunged on some lorries and driven to the docks at Liverpool. We was formed up in some sort of order and in the same order we embarked. As we went up the gangway, the dockies were trying to joke with us and more than one cracked, "There's plenty of bananas where you are going". Bananas were very scarce at that time. It made me smile, because everything was supposed to be secret.

The ship was the *Stratheden*, in peacetime a luxury and mail liner. Although it seemed haphazard the embarkation operation was remarkable. All the different trades etc were all together on the same Mess Decks. So I got to know a couple of Wireless ops fairly well. By the time things were sorted out and we had a meal, it was time to sling hammocks. That part didn't worry me, but it was amazing to see the positions some of those airmen slept in. I never knew that it was possible to sleep soundly in some of the positions I saw some in. Anyway, I suppose they did sleep and when we woke for breakfast we were not out in the wide blue sea, but in the company of a lot of other ships in a wide estuary. Whilst we were debating, a ginger haired lad joined us, took one look and said, in a very Scottish accent, "Bliddy 'ell, we are at Gurrock". Pointing to some distant cottages, he continued, "That's ma Bliddy hame. I could bliddy swim't there!"

At lunch time an RAF officer came round, calling at the tables where the WOPS was and eventually got to our table and asked, " Has any of you had any experience working with the Navy?" I put my hand up. "What experience have you had?"

"Air Sea Rescue Sir," I answered. "Good! Follow me."

So I followed him, wondering what the hell I had let myself in for. He took me to that holy of holies – the Bridge. To a Merchant navy officer there he said, "I have found you one that should be suitable, ex-Air Sea Rescue." The officer gave me the Aldis lamp, saying, "Call that ship. Say, "Dimpy fourth on column two."

I looked at him. "D-I-M-P-Y?" I asked.

"Good lad, correct spelling is D-J-Y-M-P-I, it's a Polish vessel."

I called the ship and the message was accepted. Turning to the RAF officer, the Merchant Navy Officer said, "This one will do fine. He's got a good speed."

The RAF officer left me with the officer who told me that when we was at sea the *Stratheden* would be convoy commander and all orders and signals would emanate for and from it. He also told me the watches and hours. So the following morning the huge convoy put to sea.

Out and Out, far into the Atlantic we sailed, round the north of Ireland and then turned south on what was known as a zig-zag course. Every so often, at a signal from the *Stratheden,* the whole convoy changed course like a pod of whales. That signal was done by signal flags, which were hooked on a line and then run up. I got quite adept at that, and even got that I could read these signal flags, though my main job was to signal with either the ten-inch lamp or the Aldis. Of course the job excluded me from all the other duties, including the 'Bullshit Fatigues' which meant scrubbing and polishing anything and everything possible.

When we sailed into warmer climes, I took my blanket up to the gun turret on the bridge and slept there. We put into a West African port, but nobody was allowed ashore. We were only there a brief spell and then on we sailed, round past Cape Town to Durban. There a lot of servicemen disembarked, it was said for service in North Africa.

The day before we entered Durban, I received the longest message I had ever had before. It was from our Royal navy escort ship, the County Class cruiser, the *Dorsetshire*. More of her later. The message was the order of entry into harbour and finished with the Captain of the *Dorsetshire* asking all Captains of the convoy to a special meeting and meal in Durban. The Officer on watch took the message to the Captain and returned with a message just as long, to be sent to the *Dorsetshire*. All that was visible of the *Dorsetshire* was a little blob on the horizon. I called up on the ten inch and right away she answered and I started to send. The way the signaller was receiving impressed on me that I could send faster. I speeded up so fast I could barely read my own sending and my arm was starting to tire. I was damn glad when I had finished. I would have liked to have met that signaller.

Of course, different recreations were organised to keep the troops happy and one was a boxing competition. The two wireless ops I had got friendly with told me about it and one had put his name down. His friend told me that he had beaten all comers at Yatesbury and was champion. He also said that he had entered the competition but could get no sparring partners. I said that I had done a bit, but had not put the gloves on for about four years. But I was willing to three one minute rounds with him if he could get the gloves. In a very short time he was back with the gloves and with his mate time keeping we started. It took me about three seconds to find his weak spot and at about thirty seconds, I changed from orthodox to southpaw. What we used to call left-handed. His friend called time and I had specified a thirty second rest between rounds. But there were no more rounds. The ex-champion of Yatesbury pulled his gloves off, and very surprised, I asked him why, because I was only giving him sparring taps, not hitting him hard.

"If I meet somebody like you at my weight I'll get bloody murdered," he said. Why don't *you* enter?"

"I've got more bloody sense". I said. When I was at Ramsgate, I was sparring with a lad who had entered the Southern Command boxing competition and unintentionally I caught him a blow that stopped him in his tracks. I started to apologise but he said, "never apologise when you are boxing; box on." Later that afternoon he gave me the father and mother of a boxing lesson! Meaning he pasted me!

At a later date I asked him whose stable he was in before the war. He said that he was one of Freddie Mills' sparring partners. Needless to say, he won the competition. I decided then to lead a quiet life in the RAF!

14. Arrival in India

Eventually we arrived at Bombay and a truck took us to a transit camp. The following morning we were all on parade and an Army Officer and a RAF Officer started to sort us out. in a short time, self, my two shipboard friends and two other RAF blokes were posted to Poona. An Army pickup truck took us there and eventually we arrived at Poona – in an Army camp. The following morning we went on parade. We didn't know why we were there. Five RAF in what was obviously a peacetime Army camp. When the Sergeant Major came to take the parade, he asked us what we were and when we told him RAF wireless ops, he said, "I Don't know what the hell you are doing here, but while you are I'll find something for you. Hands up those of you who can't drive." Three of us put our hands up. Pointing to me with his swagger stick, he said, "you, out here."

I marched out and looking at me, he pointed to a fifteen-hundredweight truck. "Get in that and drive it," "he said.

"But I can't drive," I said. "Don't tell me your bloody lies. I know you. You lived up Affetside. I know your mother and your Jim. I lived on Tonge Moor and was a conductor on the Affetside bus. I've seen you drive, now get in that and drive – I'll be watching you."

Luckily, the following day a RAF signals Officer came looking for five wireless operators that seemed to have gone astray. Thankfully he had found us and thankfully we said goodbye to the Army camp.

Talk about pomp and circumstance unlimited. The fact that a war was raging all over the world was not as important as the pomp and circumstance needed to impress the importance of the British RAJ. From the highest rank to the ordinary serviceman there was native servants, known as Bearers, who brought the morning cuppa, cleaned kit and would even shave you before you got up if required. Well! This signals officer took us out to a God-forsaken place out in the blue. A signals cabin and a short walk away a hut, which was our billet. We arranged wireless watches and we had the usual bearers to 'do' for us. But it was so boring. All that way, to be bored to death taking Met. Reports. I looked through the call sign book and noticed a call sign beginning MHB, so I knew that there must be Air Sea Rescue Boats somewhere. So I immediately wrote out an application for posting to ASR. I gave it to the officer and he said that he would see to it, but in the meantime I was to report to the SWO at the Parsee College, Poona.

I packed my kit and the officer himself drove me down to the college and took me to the SWO. He told me my duties – i.e. teaching Indian Officer cadets wireless and radio. Most of the cadets were Sikhs. My length of service there was roughly five hours. I took a class for three hours and then dismissed them. The monsoons had broken and they couldn't get to their rooms quick enough. The next thing they were all stripped naked, their long hair down their backs and on a kind of patio they were like a lot of kids dancing about in the rain. Then back to their dormitory. I walked in a few minutes later and there they were – in bed with each other. I called them dirty illegitimate sons, threatened to put them on charge and walked down the room, tipping them out of the beds. I went to the SWO and told him they should be put on charge. He asked me why and I told him. He asked what I did so I told him I tipped their beds up.

"Jesus Christ!" he said. "Luckily your posting has just come through to Air Sea Rescue, Chittagong, get your kit, transport will be ready to get you to the station. If you don't get away quick there'll be bloody riots. It's their religion. They believe their next leader will be born of man."

So, beating a hasty retreat, I was driven to the station, happy to know I was leaving this relic of Old British India and going once more to do what I was trained to do. My destination was 226 ASRU, Chittagong, which meant getting a train to Calcutta and then a train to Chit.

15. Calcutta

After a journey taking all day, all night and part of another day, I finally arrived at Howrah Station, Calcutta's equivalent to any of the world's biggest stations and, I think, four times more people than anywhere.

Eventually, I found the RTO (Rail Travel Officer) and there, I was told that there were no trains to Chittagong until midday the following day. I was told to go to St. James' Transit Camp.

The Sergeant saw all my kit, a tin trunk (which I still have), a kit bag, side bags etc. and said, "It's a hell of a way to carry all that, come on, I'll get you a rickshaw".

Going to the door, he shouted to one of these natives, who was in charge of a flimsy looking thing which had two flimsy wheels and shafts sticking from the flimsy box like thing.

We piled all my gear on this thing and I gingerly climbed up and sat on a frail looking seat. The sergeant said something to the rickshaw 'walla', as they were called, and then he said to me, "He'll get you there, but don't let the robbing bastard charge you more than five rupees."

So off we set, me sitting up like Lord Mukerjee and this poor devil in the shafts which I expected to see airborne any minute with the weight in the vehicle.

It seemed an awful long way to the transit camp, and I saw a lot of Calcutta before finally arriving at the camp, known as St. James's.

A bloke in the reception took me to a large dormitory style room and got two 'bearers' to carry my gear in. He told me where I could get a meal, which I found very good, and after I had cleaned up I called in his little office and asked what the entertainment was like in Calcutta and where was it possible to get a drink.

He said the only decent place where a drink was possible was a place that was the nearest thing to a servicemen's club. A place called 'The Green Shutters'.

He called a rickshaw walla and told him where to take me and said to me, "Don't give the robbing bastard more than two rupees."

I never could understand what this thing was about not overpaying the rickshaw wallas. Some years later, after I had returned to England, I heard about some demo that the rickshaw pullers staged and practically brought the city of Calcutta to a standstill.

Anyway, to The Green Shutters I rode in style and paid my charioteer the specified two rupees.

Inside were lots of servicemen, some Anglo-Indian girls, quite a few WAACI's but most important was a bar. One could get a bottle of what looked like beer and tasted like beer, but I always had my doubts.

So I sat at a table, not at all impressed, listening to a band trying to play dance music, which was awful, and watching the so-called dancers, which was worse.

Then, all of a sudden, life took on a rosier glow.

The answer was a medic who was on HSL 120 the last time I saw him. The surprise was mutual. He asked me what I was doing there. I said that I was on my way to Chit to join 226 ASRU.

He started to laugh, telling me not to bother. He was on 226 and the whole unit was in Calcutta to pick up four launches. He said they would be here for a month. He asked me where I was staying and I told him St. James's.

"Good," he said. "We are at St. James's and have our own section to ourselves. There is a bed next to mine empty. When we go back you can get your gear and join us. We have our own transport and tomorrow I'll take you to the CO."

So it was arranged and I was destined to get my first view of Chit, not from a train but from the river, on the deck of a rescue boat some four or five weeks later.

But a lot of work was necessary before that.

16. Sea Trials and Tribulations

The boats were very high-powered American launches, known as Miami launches. With two powerful Napier Marine engines with a top speed of forty plus knots. Comfortable, roomy – and a wireless cabin out of this world. But the sets, Canadian Marconi, though powerful, at first caused a real headache.

On the first sea trials we got down the river and out into the Bay of Bengal. At first my signals were clear and a good strength. Then control sent a signal, 'Your signals unreadable'. Back we went to the docks and I just could not find out why my signals should go from good to unreadable. I checked, and double-checked and my Avometer told me everything was right.

The following day, a repetition of the first. Good to start, and then gradually unreadable.

The third day I began to understand and after reading the dials on the set, I knew I could beat the Gremlin. I did a Heath Robinson job with a length of resistance wire, to the value of one Ohm. And a smooth piece of wood to act as a former. I broke the LT circuit and soldered the feeder to one end of the resistor. To the end from the set, I soldered a crocodile clip. We put to sea again and when the grid volts started to get a bit higher, I brought my heath Robinson into play with the crocodile clips.

Magic! We ran ten hours and kept a good transmission all the time, where before six hours had been the limit.

So after a week of sea trials, we could declare ourselves operational. But three other boats still had radio problems. One morning a MBC, Ginger Pearce, and a good friend of mine all the time I was out there, woke me saying, "Come on Sparks, there's an officer on deck wants a word with you."

I went on deck and this young officer said, "I want you to call base and ask for signal strength," which I did, and the answer came back 'loud and clear'.

I realised I was dealing with a signals officer, because he was reading the Morse quite easily. He wanted to know why our craft was the only one of four that was fully operational for signals.

I told him that I noticed the signals became unreadable when we had been running about six hours or so, the batteries well charged and the Grid volts rose over ten. So then I brought into play my do-it-yourself resistor.

He thanked me and said he would be back. A couple of hours later he brought some of his merry men with him and they were loaded with cameras and allsorts. They took picture of the wireless cabin, from all angles. One included a picture of your Mam I had on the desk.

He asked me if I would like to join his team. He said that he was going to Chunking soon and he could use someone like me. I said that I wouldn't mind, but I didn't think my Skipper of CO would agree. They didn't.

He sent a note with the D.R. that he was installing my resistance in the form of a rheostat and that he was sorry I couldn't join his team.

So finally we became an operational unit and away to Chittagong.

17. Chittagong and the Arakan

Almost immediately we were operating down the Arakan coast. It was not like the Channel. The distances were so huge and the area so vast it was deemed better to have the rescue boats at strategic areas on one of the islands. Of course not a bad idea, but after a length of time one got a little tired of catching fish and drinking the juice of small unripe coconuts called 'dahbs'. Besides which, the landings down the Arakan was becoming more successful, the distances back to Cal or Chit became longer but of equal distance, so Cal became the favourite. One other reason was that it was easier to refuel and the Yanks had more or less taken over Chit.

They were welcome to it. The only good or interesting thing I remember of Chit was the drums beating most of the night and at dawn the whole native population crossing the river, saying, "Nippon come." And come they did, a light Japanese air raid that would have gone unnoticed in England.

Once they made a similar raid on Calcutta and from the local newspaper reports, one would have thought that Cal had been razed to the ground. It seemed to me that India at that time never saw the war and the war to a lot was a good way of making money and to a lot of others a good way of making unimportant people important.

The Yanks started to use a warehouse very near to where we had our Base. They would offload the Liberty ships into this warehouse and on the other side of the warehouse was a railway line and the goods were loaded onto trucks for onward distribution. Ginger Pearce, a typical East Ender and a fitter from Glasgow, Jimmy Wright, were sat watching this operation of loading rail trucks. A line of coolies with turbans would walk up and an American G.I. would place a box on their heads, the coolie would do a sharp turn and walk to another G.I. on the train, who would take it from them. A sort of endless coolie belt. Overseeing all this was just one armed sentry and it took him about twenty minutes to complete his circuit. This gave our couple of bright lads and idea. They took off their bush shirts and wrapped some rag around their heads. We was all fairly well browned with the sun and in the poor light it was easy for them to make like coolies. But instead of turning to the train they quickly turned to where we were tied up. Three or four times they carried out this operation and then decided to hide the spoils – in my wireless cabin, under bunks, any place where a tin could be hidden. The wood from the cases was carried to the river mainstream where it was carried away.

The next morning, very early, the C.O and two massive American Service Police came to the boat.

"Did you leave the launch at any time last night Sparks?" the C.O. asked.

"No Sir, not at all."

"Was anyone with you?"

"Yes Sir, Ginger and Jock."

Here the Yank intervened.

"How do you know they didn't leave?" he asked.

"Because we was playing Brag and in the radio cabin you will see my winnings, if you care to look. Matches 'til we get paid."

"Well Corporal, it's queer. The patrol said he thought he saw two guys make this way." I decided to play Brag with this self-important Yank.

"Look, if the word of a British N.C.O. is not good enough, come aboard and search. I'll take it as read that you've apologised."

The Yank studied a second or so. "Beats all," he said, and walked away. Just then a D.R. came and gave the C.O., who was also our Skipper, a message. He asked for a message pad, wrote something on it and told the D.R. to give that to a certain officer. Then he said to all of us, "Make ready, we are out on a crash call." So gently we nosed out to the river, on our way down to the sea. I opened wireless watch and almost immediately HQ came up with a message for the Skipper which simply said, 'arrangement verified'. I gave it to the Skipper, who just said, "Good".

At this point I'll clarify that my two tapes had followed me out from England as a result of a quick month's course at RAF College Cranwell. Apart from the tapes, I had two years difference in back pay to come. Well down the river we went into the Bay of Bengal and crossing to the Islands of the Arakan coast. It seemed that a pilot had got into trouble but had managed to give his position before he ditched. We found the dinghy, but no airman in it and we never found him, even after two days intensive search, both at sea and on the surrounding islands, most of which were uninhabited. For every dinghy we found occupied, we found two, maybe three empty. Those waters was well populated with sharks.

Once we was looking for a reported airman down among the islands, so islands and seas were carefully combed, and having no success with the probables we started to search the improbable. More often than not, if there were natives on the island, they would disappear into the jungle, until they was certain we was not Japs. Then first to appear was the kids, then the women and then the men. On one island this happened and when the men appeared, with them was a white man, using a rough crutch and one leg roughly bandaged. He was not the pilot we was looking for, but one that was reported missing three months ago. We never found the subject of our original search.

One call, was almost a classic. The Yanks had been bombing Singapore and one of their kites had got into trouble and come down – well into Jap waters. Of course when they asked our Skipper if it was possible to pick them up, he said of course, no problem. He worked out the approximate distance, running time at full speed and how far on the return journey we can get safely before the need to refuel. So arrangements were made for a launch to meet us on the return journey, with cans of fuel to get us back to base. So off we went on an eighteen hour trip and as usual, the Skipper's navigation was spot on. There was this Yankee crew in a dinghy and there was the kite still floating. It took quite a lot of shooting with all the arms we had before it sank. The "Iron Rations" the Yanks had got off the kite were unbelievable, all of which went into our store with the other Yankee food, and cigs, which our two 'bearers' had mislaid.

The yanks thought at first we was a Jap gun boat and was quite relieved when they saw the R.A.F. roundels on the bows.

Following the usual procedure, I transmitted details to Base and then we started on our way to the American Base at Chit. Shortly after, this was about two am on Thursday, back came the signal, 'give E.T.A.' I went to the Skipper on the bridge and told that they wanted our ETA. He looked at his watch and said, "Tell them five thirty am Saturday." I made a point of remembering the time and at five thirty five AM, we dropped our American friends with their comrades. Then, loaded with American 'goodies' we sailed to our own base.

18. Unfriendly Fire

There were many landings, but one I remember was Ramree.

We was lay close inshore and about two am the gunfire seemed awful close. Then the cox bobbed his head in the cabin, saying, "Come on deck Sparks, somebody is shooting at us from a gunboat".

I went on deck with the night lamp and gave the ship-to-ship signal. They was still firing, so I used the Aldis and flashed RAF, but it was getting too warm and I started to wonder how hungry the sharks was.

One of the MBC's said "Give me your loudhailer Sparks." I found him the loudhailer and he walked to the forepeak, switched the hailer on and in his best Cockney voice shouted,

"Stop shooting you stupid bastards, we're English, RAF RESCUE CRAFT!"

They stopped shooting.

The following morning we went alongside. It was an Indian gunboat, with one white officer. He apologised to our Skipper and I asked him what was wrong with his signaller. He said "The stupid bastard had the wrong list out". He said that he was glad for once that his crew was bloody useless, otherwise we could have been blown out the water. He also said that he had not been briefed that a rescue boat would be close inshore.

Years later I heard that the Japs crossing the marsh and river close to where we was playing war with our supposed Allies. The Japs suffered severe losses. Out of a thousand men, nineteen survived. The crocs got the others.

The backup RN ship was the *Dorsetshire*. We watched her come into harbour near us and I've never felt so proud to have, in a small way, worked with her. One the foredeck, all dressed in spotless white was the Marines Band playing. It was a marvellous sight.

19. On Hill Party

A message from those faceless gods issued an edict that a convenient number of active units be sent for a rest on 'Hill Party'. The C.O. decided that, because our launch had done a lot of work and was due for a major overhaul, which would take anything up to six weeks, Ginger Pearce and Self could go on Hill Party.

Two of the crew had been on one to Darjeeling and they said it was great. So off Ginger and I set, not to Darjeeling, but a place called Shillong. A twelve-hour train journey to the railhead, in which time we emptied a large bottle of rum. At the railhead we was given a meal and told to get our heads down in a little tent until early the following morning.

Early was the operative word. At four a.m. we was given a quick breakfast and told to board the convoy of lorries waiting. Because I was a N.C.O. I was put in charge of a lorry, which meant I rode in front with the driver. A fact I didn't appreciate until later.

We started to climb into the hills immediately. Up and up, a very narrow track, twisting and turning. From tropical to sub-tropical, the vegetation changed until we was well up into the pine forests. Every so far the convoy would pull into a lay-by to allow a downward convoy to pass.

Eventually we reached our destination and I've never seen so many Service Police. They was all over the place. The reason? A very regular reaction of some of the Servicemen.

After a very awe inspiring switchback ride, one minute looking at a rock face and the next looking at a drop of hundreds of feet and seeing some wreckage where a lorry had failed to make the bend, lots of Servicemen was of the opinion that it would be better to spend their leave walking back.

This could not be allowed for several reasons. Hence the Service Police, British and American.

Near to our camp was a large American camp. Well! We was distributed among the huts, given eight blankets and told to go for more if we felt the cold. Then a talk by the M.O. who advised us to take it very easy for a week or so, owing to the rarified atmosphere.

A hunting, shooting party was arranged by the camp administrators, but after watching the way some of them handled the guns, I said to Ginger that it would be safer to go fishing. So we was given fishing tackle and off we went in this lorry.

There was only Ginger and self for the fishing party and we was the first to be dropped off at a little hut in the woods. It was well equipped and comfortable and we soon settled in.

We went to the river and tried our luck at fishing. Eventually I got a bite and what a job I had to land it. When I did land it, it was the biggest fish I had ever caught and I swear to this day the bloody thing BARKED at me. I was told it was a catfish, but I've never heard a cat bark.

We saw two natives in a boat, so I shouted to them and asked if they wanted the fish. DID THEY! So satisfied we packed up and started to make our way back to the hut.

Along the track to the hut we saw a local carrying two birds that seemed to be of the pheasant family, but bigger than any pheasant I had seen. In one hand he held a bow and on his shoulder was a quiver with about five arrows.

I managed to ask him if he had shot the birds with that equipment and he grinned. He looked at me as if he understood all about mad dogs and Englishmen. He assured us that he had. So I asked Ginger if he had an empty fag packet. He took a packet out, emptied it of the three cigarettes in it and gave me the packet and the cigarettes to our mountain Robin Hood.

When I asked him what distance he was from the birds when he shot them, he took two strides and with his fingers denoted thirty-five. At least that is what I worked out. So I measured thirty strides and put the cigarette packet in the bark of a tree. Walking back, I indicated I wanted to see him hit that.

No sooner said than done. Three arrows in that packet fast as any revolver firing. I asked him if he would sell his equipment and what did he want for it. He grinned and indicated that for five of those packets of cigs, he would trade. Fortunately Ginger had brought a good supply of smokes, so a deal was done and the hunter went away, happily smoking.

The bow was cane, the bowstring was part of the bow and the arrows were cane with sharp steel tips. Ginger and I spent the rest of our stay trying to make like deadly hunters, trying to hit two tins at twenty paces. I never counted how often we shot at the tins but a rough estimate was about two hundred shots for two hits and two would-be marksmen with bloody (literally) sore thumbs. A most remarkable fact, when we did hit the tins, the arrow went through them.

When we first arrived on camp, an officer gave us a bit of a talk. I think the Officer was with the military police. He stressed the don'ts, which were offences warranting a court martial. Don't be caught with any of the local girls, don't be seen entering or leaving a private civilian house.

The local girls were of the Khasi tribe, supposed to be among the most beautiful girls in the world and the Allied losses to these girls were greater than losses to the Japs. The servicemen went through a form of marriage with these girls and disappeared in the hills and were impossible to find.

20. Lost at Sea

Well! Our holiday was over and back we went to Base.

Our first trip was with a new Skipper whose navigation would not have got him up the Bolton-Bury canal.

After a fruitless search in what may, but most likely was not the right area he decided to return to base. Boy, did we roam about!

To make things more interesting, the sea got really nasty. The Skipper told me to get him a fix, then another, and so on every few minutes.

He said the fixes were wrong. First class three and four cross fixes, time after time. He said of the last one I got him, "Look at this, the fix puts us on top of a mountain!"

I just could not help myself, I said, "Maybe there is a mountain under the drink, but Base wants to know if we are in trouble. Have I to tell them we are probably on top of a mountain?"

Just then the fitter came out of the engine room and said, "Can you tell me how long before we reach Base, Sir?"

The Skipper said, "You had better ask Sparks, he is getting the positions, I am not sure."

The fitter said, "Somebody had better bloody find out, we are getting low on fuel."

By now the sea was getting really rough and I looked up at these damn big waves and put on my Mae West. The only time I ever did.

The Skipper disappeared below and the Cox (an ex Grimsby trawlerman) said, "Get me just one fix Sparks."

I got the fix and handed it to him. He looked at the chart, threw it to one side and got another, saying, "he even had the wrong bloody chart!"

After he checked, he took the wheel and to this day I swear he turned the launch round on one big wave. A masterful piece of seamanship.

We arrived at Base. I had previous sent ETA given to me by the Cox and what a reception committee. A Group Captain, a Wing Commander and our C.O. and I don't think it was to celebrate a good job well done.

The C.O. asked for my log book and, telling the Skipper and the Cox to go with them, they drove away in the Jeep.

The Cox was brought back in the Jeep a bit later and when we asked what had gone on he gave me my log book back, saying, "I don't think we'll be seeing THAT skipper again".

We didn't.

21. The CO's Exploits

Our next trip was another 'classic' with the C.O. as Skipper.

Again down amongst the islands and we were almost at the point of giving up when we found the pilot in the dinghy.

Ginger acted as cook and he decided to use some of our 'American friends lost rations'. A lovely dish up it was and the C.O. said, "You didn't see anyone messing around that night did you Sparks?"

"No Sir," I answered.

"Good" he said. "Ah well, for what we are about to receive, we thank the Yanks."

I often wondered if the pilot thought we were a lot of screwballs.

Months after we had picked up that American crew, we got a copy of the LIFE magazine posted to us from America. In big black type was the headline, 'Direct descendant of Drake rescues Life reporter'.

The Skipper wasn't very pleased. We knew he was a schoolmaster, we knew he was a Cornishman and did a lot of sailing for pleasure, but we didn't know his forefathers. It seemed rather strange that a Cornishman called Cook was a direct descendant of Drake.

About the last trip I did was a R.V. way down.

Things was very quiet and we was debating whether to have a swim or not. We had put the usual crash nets out and lines. Two were on the deck with rifles in case of sharks. Whilst we stood undecided, the Skipper bobbed his head out of the water saying, "What are you waiting for?" He had quietly slipped into the water, on the other side of the boat and swam under it.

Of course, that decided us.

22. A Dangerous Assignment

Just after that, the boat was once again put up on the stocks for a general overhaul and all the W.O.Ps was temporarily sent to a station called Ranchi. They was having difficulty with their signals, so we was sent to help out. We sorted out the telephone to control tower. Then got sets on frequency to the bombing range, our W.O.P.s working them.

That first day the lads were moaning and I did not blame them. WOG Pilots flying Blenheims and for every kite put on the runway, two was put on the grass.

The third day an American bomber put down and the Flying Control Office sent for me and asked me if I could get his radio on the right frequency.

I climbed into this Mitchell Bomber and got the shock of my life. Pointing through the nose of the aircraft was a bloody big cannon, belt fed. I looked at this belt, it trailed all around the aircraft in a very clever way.

Having got over that I decided to look at the set. Shades of Cranwell. It was crystal controlled, very easy to tune when you know how and easier to work, being push button.

I called control and told him all was in order. Control Officer was quite pleased, so I decided to try my luck. On the tarmac was a transport plane, and on being told it was on its way to Calcutta, I asked Flying Control Officer if there was any chance of a lift.

He just said "Yes, but you'll have to hurry, it's away in ten minutes".

I broke all records across to our billet, told one of the lads to see to my kit.

I was going to see our C.O. about getting us back where we belong.

I made it to the plane and had barely got my breath back when we was airborne.

It was no trouble to get from Calcutta airport to our base and the first person I saw was the C.O.

Somehow, I don't know why, he seemed surprised to see me.

All he said was "Well Sparks, what is it?"

I told him about the awful flying of the Indian pilots and how he would have a bunch of wireless ops with nervous disability if he didn't get them back.

He must have phoned because the next day all the WOPs was back at base.

23. Direction Finding

Only once did I ever see our C.O. at a loss.

We was running back after a perfect pick-up way down the coast.

It is not as easy as sounds, because to give you some idea, one of the messages I received more than any other was 'Ware shoals your island is uncharted'.

Well! This particular night, things was going according to plan, so the Skipper had given him the course, all he had to do was to follow the compass.

This he did very carefully and the fitter came out of the engine room for a breather, holding a big SPANNER for a natter with the cox.

So the cox followed the compass and the deck lookout gave the warning, "Breakers ahead" – then breakers to port and ditto to starboard. In fact, we were surrounded by breakers.

The Skipper was roused from his slumbers to be told of the situation. He came on deck, looked around, and we seemed to be surrounded by breakers where there should be deep water.

To Ginger he said, "Now Ginger, what would you do if you was in charge?"

Ginger grinned. "Drop the bleeding mudhook 'til daylight."

"Good," said the Skipper. "That's just what we will do."

When daylight dawned, we all wondered how the hell we had got in this lagoon of coral without damage to the boat.

Carefully the Skipper and the Cox edged out into clear sea.

Then the Skip said to me, "Now Sparks, we'll see how good that box of tricks of yours is. I want you to guide us to somewhere we know."

I switched on the RDF (Radio Direction Finding) and eventually picked up a radio beacon and the call sign told me what I had picked up.

I asked the Skipper if Patenga would be useful.

He said that would be fine.

So now, keeping my eyes on the screen (my box of tricks) with two lines making perfect cross on the Spider Line, I guided the craft for the next six hours, telling the Cox 'Port' or 'Starboard'.

Then the Skip said, "Good, that's fine Sparks. You can switch it off, I know where we are now".

So, gratefully, I switched off my box of tricks.

The only other time I had used that was in the Channel, when a bomber crew was down.

24. The Last Days of War

Some of us was sent on a updated Jungle Training course.

The instructors was two Army sergeants and an officer.

It was so much of a jungle camp that one night a tiger came into the camp and made for the cookhouse, driving the wogs mad.

We returned back from there and I finished up in hospital, my third bout of malaria after I had held it off with mepacrine and whiskey.

When I came out the Yanks had dropped The Bomb and it was expected to be the end of the war.

We lay alongside a MTB and an officer asked the cox if there was a radio op to fix their intercom as their own WOP had gone in hospital.

I went onboard and it took me ten minutes to fix it.

In the meantime someone had given me a cup of Neaters Rum.[3]

The Skipper wanted to know who had fixed the radio and when told, the RAF WOP from the Rescue boat, he ordered them to give me another cup of Neaters.

I will always remember the day the Japs packed in!

---

[3] The Rum Ration, introduced in 1740, one of the oldest traditions in the Royal Navy, was still in force during World War II.

25. Homeward Bound

So now the war was over and our thoughts turned to home and beauty.

With my release number I was the first to say goodbye to my comrades of ASRU.

First of all we had a goodbye dinner, all ranks, photos taken.

Then I took a dog I had had for two years and asked an Anglo Indian family if they would like to have him. Of course, they were glad to take him on.

So all being settled I packed my gear.

The Chippy painted my home address on my tin trunk and 'not wanted on voyage'.

So back to Bombay.

What a difference. No duties of any description. For a month, on parade at nine a.m. to be told 'That Boat' was not yet in. Free for the rest of the day.

Some of us went to the European Club called Breach Candy. Later filmed in one of Alan Whicker's TV series. There we could swim, eat and lounge about, all free.

Well, one morning we was told to get on lorries, 'That Boat', we had looked forward to for four years, was in and waiting.

What a difference on the return trip. No duties, no Bullshit parades, it was like a holiday cruise.

We came back via the Suez Canal and into the Med. We found the weather somewhat cooler, so we changed into our RAF blue and littered the Med with KD shorts, bush shirts and hats.

When coming up the Mersey one of the most glorious sights was the Liver Buildings capped with snow.

We disembarked and there was women and blokes running about with tea and sandwiches. But myself and two other lads, one from Tonge Moor and one from just outside Manchester on the Cheshire side wasn't interested. The reason being, a bottle of Scotch I had carried all the way from Calcutta for just that moment. To drink when I saw the Liver Buildings.

We entrained and was taken to Blackpool and put in civvy digs and told to parade at nine a.m. the following morning.

I put my kitbag on the bed and said to this lad from Tonge Moor, "Well I'm off." He asked me where I was going and I told him I was going home. I wasn't coming seven thousand miles to be stuck thirty miles from home.

He mentioned the parade at nine. I pointed out that there was a workman's train to Preston and from there a good bus service to Bolton. So he decided to come with me.

There was Service Police on the gates at the station and I was thinking how to talk ourselves past them with no pass. I decided to take a chance they would believe an excuse I was thinking up when we got to the gates.

They looked at our tickets and one said, "Just back from the East?"

I said we was and he just said, "OK, we have had orders not to interfere with you guys".

So on the train we got.

In Bolton a taxi and the lad from Tonge Moor was first off after arranging to meet me next morning.

But I had difficulty when I tried where I believed my home was.

No reply.

I went to the pubs where I thought my mother might be, still with the taxi, but no joy.

So I thought 'there is one solution'. I went up to our Jim's, up Affetside.

Cathy said she would show me where I lived, so into the taxi.

This time no problem.

I asked the driver to take Cathy back and how much did I owe him. He said he would take her back and there would be no charge whatsoever, seeing that I had just come back from the Far East.

I went into the house and talk about the hero's return…

My mother said "Look whose here!"

My wife, surprised, just said, "Oh! It's you!"

I met this lad the following morning and he had no better luck with his family. His eight-year-old son wouldn't speak to him.

We had to return to Blackpool to be officially demobbed and we was put on a train to Hednesford, where we was told we would finally become civilians again.

Arriving in Hednesford we was given blankets and distributed among some huts. It was winter and the huts had no heating and we spent a most miserable cold night.

The following morning, Saturday, a sergeant told us that we would go through the 'machine' that finalised our demob on Monday.

When I asked him why we had to wait until Monday, we was told that a WAAF that did some of the paperwork was on weekend leave.

I never thought I'd ever see what three hundred angry airmen could achieve!

We marched to the C.O's office and told the SWO to bring him out.

Eventually the CO came out and we wanted to know why, just because a WAAF had a weekend off, we had to starve to death until Monday in bloody cold huts.

The C.O. turned to the SWO and told him to get things moving.

The SWO told him about the WAAF on leave and the CO said if there was no one else, "Get that bloody WAAF back at once, I don't want a riot on my hands and this camp wrecked."

So things started to move.

We got papers, rail warrant, pay, medical, civvy clothes and finally the lorries ferried us to the railway station.

26. A Civilian Again

So, finally, I was back in Civvy Street.

But, like hundreds of other ex-servicemen at that time, I found it hard to settle. I switched from one job to another, until I finally settled down to lorry driving.

I got a letter from the RAF, asking me to go back with full substantive rank of sergeant. I was quite happy to do so and wrote asking about married quarters. I was told that there was a two-year waiting list for Married Quarters so I decided not to play. In two years I could be posted anywhere in the world of our fast declining Empire. So I continued trucking.

Then, some time later, the RAF decided to let me know they hadn't forgotten me and I got a letter instructing me, as a VR, to report to RAF Bow Lee, Manchester and do VR training, Tuesdays.

This was a poser to me that I pondered over whilst pounding the road.

Then I hit upon an idea. In Bolton was the Artillery Territorial Barracks, so I went there to see if I could just attend there and book in. I explained to the ADJ that I just couldn't make it to Bow Lee.

a) I hadn't a clue where it was and

b) I had no wheels to get there and

c) owing to my job, I could not be sure when I could comply.

The ADJ admitted that I had a problem and asked me what I did in the RAF.

I told him I was a WOP and RDF OP.

He said that I was just the sort of bloke they wanted in the RA and in no time I would be a sergeant.

I said that was fine, but I was still RAF.

"Oh don't worry about that," he said. "We'll see to that. Come with me."

He took me down to the signals store, pointed to a 19 set saying, "Can you set that up?"

I asked him what frequency and it took me about thirty seconds.

"Good," he said. "You'll be fine for us. Don't worry about the RAF. We'll see to that and we'll see you on Drill nights, when you can attend," he added with a smile.

So began twelve good years with the Royal Artillery Territorial Army. I got a letter from the RAF, 'Honourable Discharge. Reason for Discharge: Re-Enlistment in the R.A.T.A.'

Eventually I recieved the Territorial Efficiency Medal, to join my other gongs.

So that just about wraps up my war years and just after – just like thousands of other blokes.

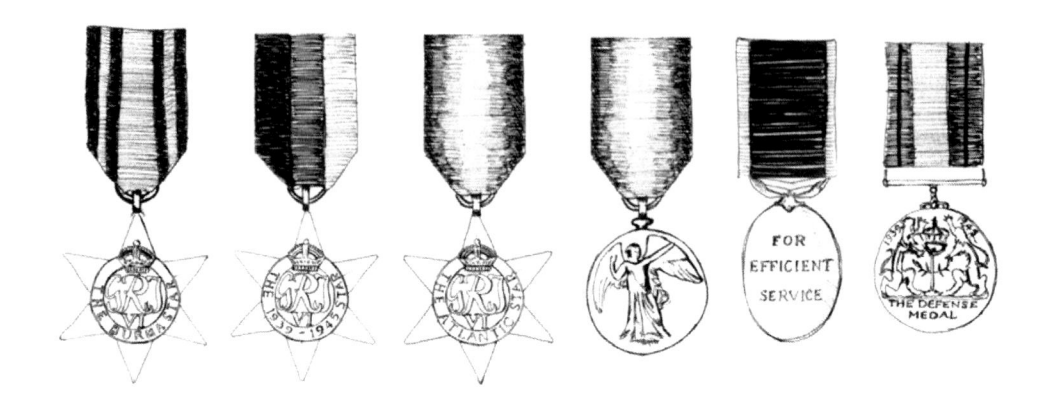

Percy's Medals: The Burma Star, The 1939-45 Star, The Atlantic Star, The Victory Medal, The Territorial Efficiency Medal and The Defence Medal

Glossary of Naval Terminology

ADJ	Adjutant – an officer assisting a superior by communicating orders
A.S.R.	Air Sea Rescue
B.E.F	Benefits Explanation Form
Chippy	Ship's carpenter
Civvy	Civilian
C.O.	Commanding Officer
E.T.A	Estimated Time of Arrival
G.D.	General Duties
H.S.L.	High Speed Launch
K.D.	Khaki Desert (shorts)
KITE	Aircraft
ME's	Messerschmitts (German Fighter Plane)
Mitchell	British Aircraft Designed by R.J. Mitchell, this includes the fighter plane the Supermarine Spitfire MK1
Mae West	Life Vest
MBC	Motor Boat Crew (Deck Hands)
MTB	Motor Torpedo Boat
MGB	Motor Gun Boat
NCO	Non Commissioned Officer
P.R.U.	Photographic Reconnaissance Unit
Queer	Strange
R.A.	Royal Artillery
R.D.F.	Radio Direction Finding Operative
R.N.	Royal Navy
R.T.O.	Rail Travel Order
R.V.	Rendezvous
SGT	Sergeant
SWO	Station Warrant Officer
WOG	Western Oriental Gentleman
WOP	Wireless Operator
W.T.	Wireless Timing Procedure
V.R.	Volunteer Reserve

Epilogue

Percy passed away a few years ago, in his late eighties, and his account of his wartime service lay forgotten until it was fortuitously unearthed many years later, thanks to his great-granddaughter's school project.

His descriptions of the many challenges and difficulties he and his colleagues faced while carrying out their air-sea rescue duties, show us that his generation did not believe in moaning about their lot – THEY JUST GOT ON WITH IT!

But what happened to HSL120? After the war, a number of the RAF's former high speed launches, built by the British Power Boat Company, Hythe, were used as houseboats in areas such as the Norfolk Broads.

Percy and Joan went on to have two more sons after the war; one of his grandsons is currently serving in Afghanistan.

Percy and Joan in their 70s.